12 Dear Lords

by Ahsilight

RoseDog Books
PITTSBURGH, PENNSYLVANIA 15238

RoseDog Books
585 Alpha Drive
Suite 103
Pittsburgh, PA 15238
Visit our website at *www.rosedogbookstore.com*

ISBN: 979-8-89027-247-8

eISBN: 979-8-89027-745-9

12 Dear Lords

I dedicate this book to ¨The World¨
To All that I have encountered along the way.
To the present and future!

I decided to start you, my journal, so I will have someone to tell my emotions to and maybe try to comprehend what is going on with me. I have decided to love and not to hate. I think it will get me further.

Journal Entry # 1

Dear Lord why, why, why do you keep letting me be around people and men that do not love nor care about me? They lie and make me feel humiliated and I cannot take it anymore. Please keep everybody out of my life that means me harm, no good, wants to use me or hurt me.

Dear Lord, so much injustice has been done to your child that I do not even feel like a real person anymore. I do not know any real people and everybody hates me. Dear Heavenly Father, deliver me from my life. I have to believe that God has me going through what I am going through for a reason. In the Bible it says you have not because you ask not. I ask for love given and received.

Dear Heavenly Father
How many times must my heart break and how many times must my soul cry out? I am tired and I cannot take it anymore. Everybody that I get close to abandons me and I have love but no trust. Dear Lord, please surround me with good caring people that genuinely love, intend and mean good.

Why Lord Why?

Journal Entry # 2

All I have is love and that gets me hurt every time. I am so angry and so hurt that I do not know what to do. I am lost and feel like I will never be found. I am empty and feel like I will never be filled. I am always deceived by wolves in sheep's clothing. Take me away O Lord from people that deceive me and mean me harm. Take me away O Lord from people that despise me and hate me. Take me away O lord from everyone, because no one loves the way I love. I am close to no one and every one is mean to me, and makes me feel stupid. Take me away O lord from evil deceitful people. Everyone turns their back on me as if I were not a real person. Everybody takes my kindness for weakness. Everybody walks all over me, I am a doormat.

I have never known real true love between a man and a woman, or anybody else for that matter. I wonder does it even exist? I am a lost sheep yearning to find my way home. I am always protected, I feel that from the presence of the Lord, but my feelings aren't. They are crushed and trampled on every time. I feel like a fool all the time. I have no Man to call my own, no one am I close to in my family and no friends either. I am just a stupid nice person who no one cares about. WOW

Ahsilight

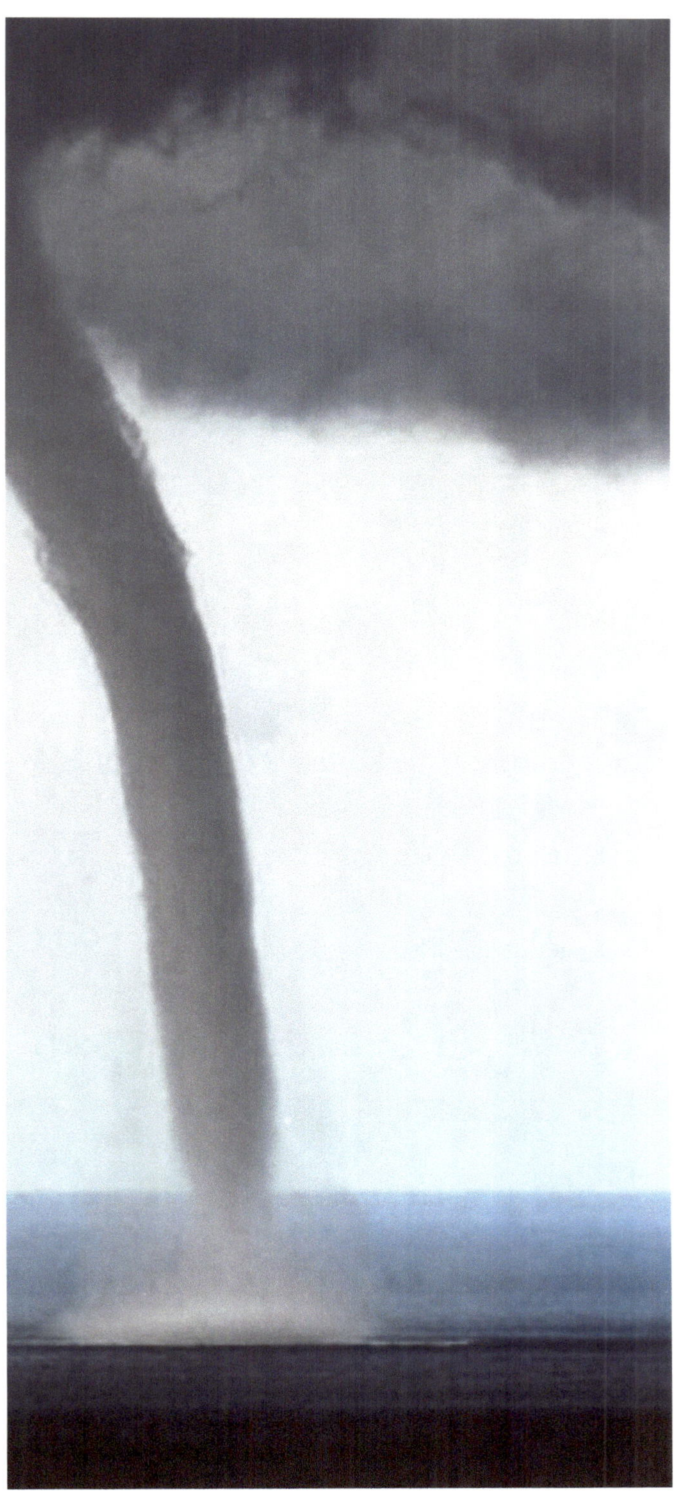

Journal Entry # 3

No person alive can I trust. I am so scared. I am so all alone. I am so secluded. Everybody knows more about me than I do and it is going on in my face. But God made me this way, He knew me before I knew myself. Dear Lord, please forgive me for my sins, and wash me clean as snow. Dear Journal, that is why you are my new best friend, because you cannot hurt me. All you are, is my words, my thoughts, my feelings on paper.

Y does the world forsake me? Y do people eat away at my soul? Y is life so painful? Deliver me O Lord, I am in a world full of strangers. Everybody in my life deserts me. Y must I continually suffer at the hands of others? Separate me o lord from the wicked, protect me from injustice. Heal my broken heart and tarnished body. Touch me with your goodness, fill me with your peace. Protect me like a precious stone protected from the fire. Heal me, save me and keep me righteous in your sight, so that I may enter into your precious Kingdom where I will be safe from harm forever and ever.

Journal Entry # 4

Maybe one day I will know what it is like to love another human being and what it is like to have a human being love me. But for now Lord I do not know what a love between two people is like, somehow I always get the short end of the stick. I do not remember when it started happening. Dear Lord please give me the strength to withstand all the trials, tribulations and deceit the devil has in store for me. Dear Heavenly Father, teach me how to walk, talk and pray.

- Loneliness
- Oneness
- Virtue
- Eternal

Dear Heavenly Father,
Although this is a journal, I feel like I am talking to you when I write. Heal my mind, heal my conscience, heal my soul. Help me not to disobey you and at the same time honor your name. Help me to grow close to you through the gift of the Holy Spirit, so that I may be blessed and a blessing to others and to you o God. Help me to be delightful to you in all my ways and please direct my footsteps. Please heal me inside and out Lord. I cast all my cares onto you. I give you my burdens. I praise your Holy Name!

Ahsilight

Journal Entry # 5

"For I know the plans I have for you," Declares the Lord, "plans to prosper you and not to harm you, plans to give you hope and a future." Jeremiah 29:11

First I want to give thanks to my Heavenly Father and Jesus Christ for coming into this world, and setting an example. Also dying on the cross for my sins and giving me a connection through the Holy Spirit to Father God. I have never had a real dad so abba Father. You are my one and only true dad and Father.

Throughout the years I have suffered greatly but as God said, he does not put more on you than you can bear. My memory of things has been eased over the years, and I am a true believer that time heals all wounds.

Journal Entry # 6

I just feel so poor like I am a bumb and like I be bothering people. I really feel all alone like I have no friends, but I know Jesus is my friend. Even though the devil tries to attack me and the people that are close to me turn their back on me, I shall not be moved. Dear Lord, you know that I went to school to get a career so that everything would turn out right, but my mental illness took its toll and now I am living off of disability and that is exactly what it is disabling. Please help me Lord, let your light shine on me and let me stay away from people.

Journal Entry # 7

All of my friends have been taken from me. I am so sad, I hate being needy and having people punk me. To me being broke is a crime, It's like it gives people the right to treat you any kind of way. I have been scraping tobacco off the carpet all day. Dear Lord, please take care of me and prosper me. O lord please do not leave me out in the cold. I thank you, I love you and I trust you!

Dear Lord, please help me not to be discouraged, misled, or misbehaved. Thankyou Lord for myself, you have never left me nor forsaken me. Thankyou for my family. It is very huge so there is always someone to love you when you need it. Thank you for you Lord.

Ahsilight

Journal Entry # 8

I know there is a God and I know he is all powerful and because I know this I cannot take no more. I know God has the power to free me from this imprisonment and he also has the power to help me but he doesn't. My pain, anguish and loneliness grows more and more everyday. I have suffered so many years and I am not going to fight anymore.

There is no one in my corner and God knows this. People act like they are, but everybody I know has something to say about the next person when they are as selfish and greedy as the next person. If I could run away I would but I have ran my whole life and mental illness, selfish people and evil is not something you can run from. Dear Lord, please protect me and keep me away from harm.

YESHUA

Journal Entry # 9

Everybody I know is a hater, everybody stabs me in the back over and over. Well I am not taking the knife out this time. I am going to die with it and God can remove it. He is the only one who can save my soul.

And Joy cometh in the morning,,, Thankyou Lord, thankyou Heavenly Father, please help me to deal with my struggles and not commit suicide. Please heal me inside and out. Please strengthen my mind Lord and strengthen my body. Please fill me with your spirit so that I may be pleasing in your sight. Please help me to help myself and those that need help also. Dear Lord, please direct my footsteps and teach me how to walk, talk and stay in your will.

Journal Entry # 10

Thankyou Lord for making me the way that I am, because I know I was made this way for a purpose. Thankyou for my teenage years before I developed a mental illness. I know I have potential. Dear Lord, please help me to be a better Individual. Thankyou for your son Jesus Christ. Please help me to remember that the Holy Spirit dwells in me and "Greater is he that is in me than he that is in the world."

Please wipe every tear from every eye lord, and help mankind to get along. Dear Lord, please accept me into your eternal gates of joy. For you did not give me a spirit of fear, but one of love, peace, joy and a sound mind. And this too shall pass as they say but in the meantime☐ Dear Lord, will you give me the strength to make it through?

Ahsilight

Journal Entry # 11

Dear Heavenly Father, please take care of me and everybody I love, even the people I do not. Please take care of all of my enemies also. Please grow me up in you and help me to live up to your standard. Please keep me safe, watch over me and help me to forgive.

Dear Lord please let me see me as you see me. Please make me aware of my faults so that with your help my paths may be made straight and I will choose the narrow path that leads to righteousness and not the wide one that leads to destruction. You sat before me life or death, I choose life for your word says your yoke is easy and your burdens are light. Protect me O lord keep me safe and in your will.

JESUS

Journal Entry # 12

Dear Lord I know that you know me inside and out and because you know me I know you know what is in my heart. I have always wanted a husband, a man of my own. In your word it says a woman is to her husband, her husband to Christ and Christ to God. So how can I be wrong to yearn for a husband? How can I be wrong to yearn for male companionship, attention and support? I cast all my cares on you Lord I know you will work it out.

Ahsilight

www.ingramcontent.com/pod-product-compliance
Lightning Source LLC
Chambersburg PA
CBHW040903110726
48005CB00001B/182